# Stories
# to Learn and Live by
True Animal Stories, the Bible, and the ABCs of Life

by

Annie M. Burton

Copyright © Annie M. Burton

All rights reserved. No part of this publication may be reproduced, distributed, or transmitted in any form or by any means, including photocopying, recording, or other electronic or mechanical methods, without the prior written permission of the publisher, except in the case of brief quotations embodied in critical reviews and certain other noncommercial uses permitted by copyright law.

All Scripture are taken from the King James Version of the Bible.

US Copyright registration TX-8-976-794

ISBN-978-1-951300-16-6

Liberation's Publishing LLC
West Point - Mississippi

# Stories
## to Learn and Live by
True Animal Stories, the Bible, and the ABCs of Life

**Adopt a pet from your nearest animal shelter!**

# Contents

Introduction ............................................................. 1

Animals of The Bible ............................................... 3

Smokie ...................................................................... 5

Snowball ................................................................... 7

Our Dog Spot ........................................................... 9

Slaughter ................................................................ 11

Sam, A Tabby with A Mission .............................. 13

The Bunny Family ................................................. 17

Lady and Missy ..................................................... 19

Three Pet Pigeons ................................................. 21

Little Black Bear ................................................... 23

Kitty Poo and Sylvester ........................................ 25

Jo Jo and Buuke .................................................... 27

Big Fish in A Small Pond ..................................... 29

Lily .......................................................................... 31

Sugar ...................................................................... 33

The Bible ................................................................ 35

The Lord's Prayer ................................................. 39

The 23rd Psalm ............................................................... 40

Psalm Ninety-One............................................................ 41

The Ten Commandments .................................................. 43

How to Be Saved from Your Sins ...................................... 45

The Sinners Prayer ........................................................... 46

How to Stay Saved ............................................................ 47

The Seven Things God Hates ........................................... 48

The A B C's of Life ........................................................... 49

Children are Gifts from God ............................................. 53

My Friend, CeCe .............................................................. 55

Courage and Social Justice ............................................... 57

Resurrection Day Song ..................................................... 61

About the Author .............................................................. 67

Intervention Crisis Hotline Numbers ............................... 71

# Dedication

This book is dedicated to many children, grandchildren, and great grandchild, Kyla, who shared her story about her pet turtle Lily.

*My children are Henry, Ruby and Jacqueline. Michael, Gwendolyn, and Catherine. Debra, Katrina, Ray and Kyland. Jackie, Jassica, Derek, Kayla, Peggy and great grandchild.*
*Much love to all of you. Enjoy the reading, you will be blessed.*

May the Lord guide your lives and continue to bless you in a special way. You are my heart and I love you very much. Stay with God. He will never leave you.

Annie M. Burton

# **Introduction**

What I want readers to take from this book is for the youth to get back to the joy of reading and the effect reading has on your life. When you read you acquire knowledge, and it is stored in your memory bank to be recalled again when needed. It is a gift from God. There is no other gift like it. You don't have to be an introvert.

We have been shut in on account of COVID19, which causes some depression. You don't have to stay depressed. Reading can change your thinking and turn your negative thoughts into positive ones. The most read book in the world is the Holy Bible. It's the number one best seller. When you read your Bible, you learn more about who God really is. He loves us. Who else would send their son to die on the cross for the sins of the world? He loves us unconditionally. Read your Bible

In your Bible you learn God created all things, man, and animals, great and small. He also created the universe, the sky, moon, sun, stars, clouds, and the planets, which includes the earth, mars, mercury, Venus, Saturn, Uranus, Jupiter, Neptune, and Pluto.

Then out of the ground the Lord formed every beast of the field and every fowl of the air and brought them to Adam to see what he would call them. Whatsoever Adam called them that was the name of every living creature that God had made. Gen. 1:19 (KJV)

The purpose of this book is to get both children and adults to read more. Reading is a skill like no other. People are getting away from it. There are so many stories to be read that have never been told.

In my book there are sixteen true stories and I hope every reader be blessed and enjoy the contents. There is other information from the Bible that is helpful to all. There are also some facts of life's how to be courageous, and social justice affects everyone. We need to be watchful and prayerful as we live our lives daily.

Let us find ourselves caring for each other, loving one another more, helpers one to another and love God with all our heart, mind, soul, will, and strength. This book closes with a song/ play "He arose". Jesus arose from the dead. It is the best thing that has happened to us. Read your bible.

This book is recommended for children's church.

## **Animals of The Bible**

And the Lord said unto Noah, come thou and all thy house into the ark. For thee I have seen righteous before me in this generation. Of every clean beast thou shalt take to thee by sevens, the male, and his female: and of beasts that are not clean by two, the male and his female. Of fowls also of the air by sevens, the male and female: to keep seed alive upon the face of all the earth. Genesis 7:1-3 KJV.

And they brought the colt to Jesus and cast their garments on him: and he sat upon him. Mark 11:7. KJV

And the Lord opened the mouth of the ass, and she said unto Balaam, what have I done unto thee, that thou hast smitten me these three times? Numbers 22:28 KJV

Annie M. Burton

## **Smokie**

When I was age three, my dad had a bull called Smokie. We had a large yard front and back with large trees. I liked to play under the trees. My brother Joe liked to play under the trees too.

Smokie was kept in the back yard with a chain. My brother played mostly in the back. He was not afraid of the bull. When I was in the backyard Smokie would run towards me. I was afraid of him. I don't think he liked me. Smokie would stomp his feet and snort and I would run away. I would go and play in the front yard away from him where it was quiet. I told my mother Smokie did not like me. Sometimes my dad would put him in the truck and take him away. I was so glad. While he was gone, I could play without being afraid. Sometimes he would be gone for a long time.

That was alright with me. The neighbors would give us milk and butter, and I liked that. Finally, my dad sold Smokie, and I was so glad. I was not afraid to play in the yard anymore. I never saw him again. But I remembered his long horns and mean look.

Annie M. Burton

## **Snowball**

When I was a student nurse, one of my classmate's dog had a litter of puppies that she was giving away. We got a small, white, fuzzy, little house pet. We named her snowball. Her fur was as white as snow. She was so much fun to play with. She was my children's first pet. Everyone in the neighborhood loved snowball. The children would come over every day and play at our house.

Our house burned, and we had to live with another family. We could not bring snowball inside, so she stayed outside. One night after playing with her. The children came inside. And that was the last time we saw her. The next morning, we looked for her but couldn't find her. She was gone. Someone had taken her away. We missed her. All the children missed her. We never saw her again. I hoped she had found a good home. I hoped she was taken care of. She was such a good pet and deserved the best care.

Annie M. Burton

## Our Dog Spot

After the house fire, the family bought a home in another community in a new subdivision. We moved in. We met new friends and new neighbors. So many people came to see us and helped us out. Even strangers from far and near wished us well with many gifts like clothing, furniture, food, dishes, household items and money. We had so much there wasn't enough room to keep it all. We had to give some things away. I thanked God for how everyone was so kind and sharing.

A man from the animal shelter came by and wanted to know if we wanted to adopt a puppy. He had several with him. We said, "yes" and chose the black and white one. We called him spot. He was a small terrier, very friendly and energetic. Spot thought he was a big dog. He would run and play with the larger dogs. He would get in fights that he could not win. At that time there would be a lot of pets running free in the area and Spot would join them. I was afraid for him since he was so small. He was an outside pet.

He would get into fights all the time. The last one he was in was really bad. He was sick for a long time and did not recover. We all missed him when he was gone.

Annie M. Burton

## **Slaughter**

Slaughter was a large black lab and our neighbor's pet. He was the neighborhood dog too, and he went from house to house. Children and parents both loved him. He would eat wherever he went. Once when that family took him to the vet, he was given some type of medication. It changed him from the mild-mannered lab he was to a very vicious dog. We could no longer play with him. He was so different. He became dangerous. That was so sad. We lost the neighborhood pet who was so loving and mild mannered that you could not help but love. You could hug and cuddle him, play ball, race down the street. But not anymore. We were afraid he would bite us. We really don't know what caused him to change. Everyone missed playing with him.

Annie M. Burton

## **Sam, A Tabby with A Mission**

Sam was a large yellow and white tabby that belonged to my daughter. He was a wonderful house pet. Sam would walk down the street with you just like a pet puppy. One day Sam disappeared from the house, and no one knew where he was. He was gone for a very long time, and the family thought they would never see him again. They also wondered had anyone else taken him away. Finally, one day Sam came back, but he was not alone. He brought home a wife and a kitten. My daughter named the kitten Charley, and he grew up to be a very large cat.

Somehow a raccoon caught Charley and broke off one of his hind legs. Even though he lost one half of his leg, it did not handicap him at all. He managed to do very well and maintain his activities without any setbacks. He is still with the family today. Sam and his wife are gone.

The family would go on vacation in the early spring to Canada. We always had to cross the Border and have our passports ready. Even Charley had to have his papers and immunization records ready. Sometimes it would take such a long time to go across the border three to four hours to get across. Then we would come to the offices of exchange where we exchange our money for spending. We rented cabins on the lake and fished every day. The weather was fine the fishing was great. My daughter and son-in-law would rent pontons for us to fish on. We always left Charley in the cabin. My granddaughter loved fishing.

She was young and liked to swim. Sometimes when we were coming into the shore, she would jump off of the boat and swim to the shore. She learned to swim at an early age.

We always went to Canada during the bass season. Everyone always caught fish and had a fish fry. After the fish fry we would go into the cities and shop. The stores had all kinds of souvenirs. They had cups, tee shirts, keychains, balls, balloons flip flops, glasses, note pads, scarfs, I cannot name them all. We would always bring things back for other family members, friends, church members and co-workers. When we return from fishing to cross the border, we had to show our fish we caught in the coolers. It was all fun after that it was a long ride home. Charley would ride in our laps from one to the other

Canada is a beautiful country to visit and take a vacation. I'll never forget the times I visited, different cities like Toronto, Harwood, and cowbird. Beautiful cities and a beautiful country. Canada is known for its lakes and fisheries. The landscape is an awesome site to see. While riding along the interstate and highways you can see eagles flying above the trees. Some eagles build their nests on the utility poles right beside the highways and you can see the eagle were smaller. They were not bald eagles. So, we called them Canadian eagles. There were other utility poles that were power sources. They also supplied certain types of energy. There was no nest built on those poles, only the ones near the roadways. I suppose they liked having a bird's eye view. Eagles have two sets of eyelids, one they shut down and see through and use while flying to protect their eyes. The bald eagle is the symbol of power. The bald eagle is the largest of all eagles. It is the national bird of the United States of America.

Annie M. Burton

## **The Bunny Family**

One night the family picked up their grandson from work at around midnight. Upon arrival at the house turning into the driveway they saw a family of three rabbits crossing the street and came into the yard. They stopped and he took out his phone and began to take pictures of them. They were not afraid. The bunnies stopped at the moment and then continued on to where they were going under the shrub is where they lived.

The next day they were gone, but you could see the place was where they had lived and made themselves comfortable. Their living habitat has gone undisturbed until this day.

Annie M. Burton

## **Lady and Missy**

Lady was a collie with class, and missy a chihuahua was her little friend. They lived together in a mansion on a prominent street in the city. The owner of the house had a carpentry business. They both would ride around the city together in a luxury car. Lady was quiet and laid back. Missy was energetic and barked a lot. There was never a quiet time with missy.

They would take long rides in the country with their heads out of the car window, the wind blowing their ears. Both missy and lady were well trained how to meet house guests. Lady was a gentle giant that weighed over fifty pounds. She was fine with sharing the house with missy. The same bed and the same food. They got along better than some people. They were two great watch dogs.

Annie M. Burton

## **Three Pet Pigeons**

The Family caught three pigeons and wanted to make pets out of them. They were put in a safe enclosure off the ground and fed several times a day. There was limited flying space for them. The birds could become carrier pigeons with the correct training. We did not know where to begin with that project. We kept the birds away from other animals. They were very interesting, always cooing. Pigeons are wild birds and should live in the wild. So, we set them free.

Annie M. Burton

## **Little Black Bear**

The day the little black bear came to town. There was so much excitement. It came through our neighborhood into different neighbors' yards, around their storage sheds. He just kept going through the subdivision maybe looking for food.

The bear left our neighborhood and went to another neighborhood. We got in the car and followed it, to see where it would go. People were coming out of their houses; children were all excited and following the bear as it went from one area to another.

It probably was afraid of us. So, it went toward the highway. There were some tall trees there and it decided to climb one of the trees. It went almost to the top. Someone called the fire department and veterinarian. The fire department spread their net and the vet tranquilized the bear. It fell into the net and was carried away. That has not happened before. That was the first time something like that happened.

Annie M. Burton

# Kitty Poo

# Sylvester

## **Kitty Poo and Sylvester**

Kitty poo is a grey and white feline, very beautiful and sixteen years old. Living with her owners all these years. She has had some litters at different times. Her kittens were adopted by friends and family members.

Another tabby came and began living outside. The family thought she was a girl. So, they called her Sylvia. For many years Sylvia lived outside and she would hunt small animals like a dog. She is a very large dark smoked grey animal. Very quiet and likes to sit alone. One day she became ill. The family took her to the vet and discovered she was a boy. So, they named him Sylvester. He continues to hunt small animals and kitty poo still lives at the residence. They see the vet when ill.

## **Jo Jo and Buuke**

JoJo and Buuke are two fine horses living on their owner's ranch. JoJo is a male and Buuke is a female. They are two gentle giants. These two horses are on the gates that welcome you to the ranch. These two animals are family friendly, mild mannered, and a pleasure to be around. Children like to go horseback riding.

There is always work to be done to care for the animals. Horses are the most valuable and faithful of the four-legged animals to man. Besides feeding, watering, shearing, grooming, and replacing horseshoes and hoof care they are man's livelihood. They are very strong work animals. They can till the ground, carry heavy loads, travel, and herd cattle. Horses perspire and are given a block of salt to replace the electrolytes they have lost while working or from being in the hot sun.

However, when all the work is done comes the pleasure of horseback riding. When horses become ill, they see the veterinarian. Also do not forget to clean the stalls.

Annie M. Burton

## Big Fish in A Small Pond

There is a fishpond on the same ranch with the horses. There are big fish in this small pond. The ranch is so beautiful with shrubs, flowers, fruit and flower trees and vegetable gardens. The pond is located in the rear. People are allowed to fish and keep their catch. Fishing is a good sport. It's also relaxing and enjoyable. It puts food on the table. Fish can be processed and prepared and served as fillet, fish sticks, nuggets. It can be served as fried fish, broiled, and tuna sandwiches. It's all good. Fish can swim for miles in rivers, lakes, oceans, ponds, upstream and downstream. The ones that live in ponds are maintained in their own habitat.

Annie M. Burton

## **Lily**

Lily was a house pet turtle that lived in a town house with her owner. She was a small gray turtle. So, shy she would hide in her adobe to keep away from people. Her color allowed her to blend in with the rocks and bridge in her tank. Sometimes her owner would take Lily out of her house to get exercise. Her house was upstairs. She would head for the stairs, sometimes tumbling down the steps heading for the front door that was at the end of the stairs and wanted to go outside. Just like she knew where she was going. There are over two hundred species in the world. They can live in fresh or salt water. Others live on land or partly in water. They breathe with lungs. The females lay eggs in large amounts. Some turtles live to be over one-hundred years old. Lily's family relocated to another state. They took her to a pond and released her. Perhaps sad about leaving her behind, her owner hoped she would be happy at that pond.

Annie M. Burton

## Sugar

Sugar is a small house dog, a pug mixed. A girl with a tan coat and a dark brown face. Very energetic and likes to eat. She likes her snacks better than her food. Sugar does not like to take baths. After the bath when she gets dry. She likes to run through the house doing canine sprints until she gets too tired to run. I started teaching her how to jump through hoops. She did a few jumps but did not like it. What sugar does to relax is to sunbath on the patio. She also likes to go frog hunting in the backyard. I don't see any more out there, so I suppose she ran them all away. Sometimes birds fly down in the yard and eat bugs and worms. She tries to catch them too. Sugar likes to visit doggie daycare and walk in the park with the other pets. A day at the vet is alright with her. She takes her shots like a brave little pet. She enjoys riding looking out of the window.

Annie M. Burton

# **The Bible**

I pledge allegiance to the Bible, God's Holy word. It is a lamp unto my feet and a light unto my path. I hide His word in my heart that I might not sin against God.

The Bible is the written and inspired word of God. God inspired holy men to write it. There are sixty-six books in the bible. Thirty-nine in the Old Testament and twenty-seven in the New Testament.

## The first five books are in the Old Testament is the law.
Genesis
Exodus
Leviticus
Numbers
Deuteronomy

## The next twelve books are History.
Joshua
Judges
Ruth
I Samuel
II Samuel
I Kings
II Kings
I Chronicles
II Chronicles
Ezra
Nehemiah
Esther

## The next five books are poetry.
Job		Psalm
Proverbs	Ecclesiastes
Song of Solomon

## The next five books- Major Prophets
Isaiah
Jeremiah

Lamentations
Ezekiel
Daniel

<u>The next twelve books-Minor Prophets</u>
Hosea
Joel
Amos
Obadiah
Jonah
Micah
Nahum
Habakkuk
Zephaniah
Haggai
Zechariah
Malachi

<u>The New Testament contains twenty-seven books.</u>

<u>The Four Gospels</u>
Matthew
Mark
Luke
John

<u>The early Church established the Acts of the Apostles.</u>
Acts

## Twenty-One Epistles
Romans
I Corinthians
II Corinthians
Galatians
Ephesians
Philippians
Colossians
I Thessalonians
II Thessalonians
I Timothy
II Timothy
Titus
Philemon
Hebrews

## New Testament contains
James
I Peter
II Peter
I John
II John
III John
Jude

## Prophecy
Revelation

# The Lord's Prayer
Matthew 6:9-13

Our Father which art in heaven, hallowed be thy name. Thy kingdom come, Thy will be done in earth, as it is in heaven. Give us this day our daily bread. And forgive us our debts, as we forgive our debtors. And lead us not into temptation but deliver us from evil: For thine is the kingdom, and the power, and the glory, forever. Amen.

# The 23rd Psalm

1 The Lord is my shepherd; I shall not want.

2 He maketh me to lie down in green pastures: he leadeth me beside the still waters.

3 He restoreth my soul: he leadeth me in the paths of righteousness for his name's sake.

4 Yea, though I walk through the valley of the shadow of death, I will fear no evil: for thou art with me; thy rod and thy staff they comfort me.

5 Thou preparest a table before me in the presence of mine enemies: thou anointest my head with oil; my cup runneth over.

6 Surely goodness and mercy shall follow me all the days of my life: and I will dwell in the house of the Lord forever.

## **Psalm Ninety-One**

Read every day. It is our protection.

1 He that dwelleth in the secret place of the most High shall abide under the shadow of the Almighty.

2 I will say of the Lord, He is my refuge and my fortress: my God; in him will I trust.

3 Surely he shall deliver thee from the snare of the fowler, and from the noisome pestilence.

4 He shall cover thee with his feathers, and under his wings shalt thou trust: his truth shall be thy shield and buckler.

5 Thou shalt not be afraid for the terror by night; nor for the arrow that flieth by day;

6 Nor for the pestilence that walketh in darkness; nor for the destruction that wasteth at noonday.

7 A thousand shall fall at thy side, and ten thousand at thy right hand; but it shall not come nigh thee.

8 Only with thine eyes shalt thou behold and see the reward of the wicked.

9 Because thou hast made the Lord, which is my refuge, even the most High, thy habitation;

10 There shall no evil befall thee, neither shall any plague come nigh thy dwelling.

11 For he shall give his angels charge over thee, to keep thee in all thy ways.

12 They shall bear thee up in their hands, lest thou dash thy foot against a stone.

13 Thou shalt tread upon the lion and adder: the young lion and the dragon shalt thou trample under feet.

14 Because he hath set his love upon me, therefore will I deliver him: I will set him on high, because he hath known my name.

15 He shall call upon me, and I will answer him: I will be with him in trouble; I will deliver him, and honour him.

16 With long life will I satisfy him, and shew him my salvation.

# The Ten Commandments

Exodus 20:3-17

3 Thou shalt have no other gods before me.

4 Thou shalt not make unto thee any graven image, or any likeness of anything that is in heaven above, or that is in the earth beneath, or that is in the water under the earth.

5 Thou shalt not bow down thyself to them, nor serve them: for I, the Lord thy God am a jealous God, visiting the iniquity of the fathers upon the children unto the third and fourth generation of them that hate me;

6 And shewing mercy unto thousands of them that love me and keep my commandments.

7 Thou shalt not take the name of the Lord thy God in vain; for the Lord will not hold him guiltless that taketh his name in vain.

8 Remember the sabbath day, to keep it holy.

9 Six days shalt thou labour, and do all thy work:

10 But the seventh day is the sabbath of the Lord thy God: in it thou shalt not do any work, thou, nor thy son, nor thy daughter, thy manservant, nor thy maidservant, nor thy cattle, nor thy stranger that is within thy gates:

11 For in six days the Lord made heaven and earth, the sea, and all that in them is, and rested the seventh day: wherefore the Lord blessed the sabbath day, and hallowed

it.

12 Honour thy father and thy mother: that thy days may be long upon the land which the Lord thy God giveth thee.

13 Thou shalt not kill.

14 Thou shalt not commit adultery.

15 Thou shalt not steal.

16 Thou shalt not bear false witness against thy neighbour.

17 Thou shalt not covet thy neighbour's house, thou shalt not covet thy neighbour's wife, nor his manservant, nor his maidservant, nor his ox, nor his ass, nor any thing that is thy neighbour's.

## **The Plan of Salvation**
How to Be Saved from Your Sins

Repent from your sins.
Turn away from them.
Believe in your heart and confess with your mouth.
**Romans 10:9** That if thou shalt confess with thy mouth the Lord Jesus, and shalt believe in thine heart that God hath raised him from the dead, thou shalt be saved.

**Romans 10:10** For with the heart man believeth unto righteousness; and with the mouth confession is made unto salvation.

**Romans 10:13** For whosoever shall call upon the name of the Lord shall be saved.

**Acts 4:12** Neither is there salvation in any other: for there is none other name under heaven given among men, whereby we must be saved.

## **The Sinners Prayer**

Dear Lord Jesus,
I am a sinner. I come to you to ask you to forgive me of my sins. I believe you are the son of God. I believe you died on the Cross for my sins. I repent for every sin I every committed. I am sorry Lord for sinning against you. Save me now. I make you the Lord of my life. I want to live for you from this day forward and write my name in the Lamb's Book of Life.

Amen

## **How to Stay Saved**

Leave the old sinful life behind. Live righteous, pray, and read your bible every day. Ask the Lord for help to understand his word. Get in a church that's teaching the Gospel of Jesus Christ. Love God with all of your heart, and love your neighbors as yourself.

II Corinthians 5:17 Therefore, if any man be in Christ, he is a new creation; old things have passed away; behold, all things have become new.

## **The Seven Things God Hates**

### **Proverbs 6:16-19**

16 These six things doth the Lord hate: yea, seven are an abomination unto him:

17 A proud look, a lying tongue, and hands that shed innocent blood,

18 A heart that deviseth wicked imaginations, feet that be swift in running to mischief,

19 A false witness that speaketh lies, and he that soweth discord among brethren.

## **The A B C's of Life**

**A-Angels:** spiritual beings dwelling in heaven, employed as ministering spirits or agents of God for his people.

**B-Baptism:** to immerse in water after receiving Jesus Christ as our Savior after repenting from our sins.

**C-Church:** a local assembly of baptized believers who have been redeemed and follow Jesus Christ as Savior and Lord.

**D-Decree:** an order having the force of Law when you pray. You can decree a thing and it shall be established or done.

**E-Eden:** a garden eastward in Eden where Adam and Eve first lived.

**F-Faith:** our belief in God. The just shall live by his faith.

**G-God:** the creator of all things, man, animal, and the Universe. The Supreme Being.

**H-Holy:** the state of being righteous set apart for the master's use.

**I-Idol:** a false god; idolatry

**J-Jesus:** the son of God, the anointed one who gave his life on the cross for our sins.

**K-Kingdom of God:** it is love, joy and peace in the Holy Ghost.

**L-Love:** we have love one to another by this all men will know we are Christ's disciples. For God is love.

**M-Master:** Jesus was called Master by his disciples

**N-Nahum:** a short prophetic book of the Old Testament that tells the destruction of the nation of Assyria and its capital city Nineveh.

**O-Obedient:** to carry out the word or will of another person especially the will of God.

**P-Prayer:** communicating with God. A petition of what one needs, giving thanks to God.

**Q-Queen of Sheba:** a queen who came to visit Solomon, the King of Israel who tested him with hard questions and found that his wisdom and prosperity exceeded his fame.

**R-Repent:** turning away from sin, rebellion and disobedience and turn back to God and forsake your sin.

**S-Sabbath:** a day of rest and worship.

**T-Tabernacle:** the tent which served as a place of worship for the nation of Israel during their early history.

**U-Unity:** when the believers were all with one accord in one place on the day of Pentecost in the upper room.

**V-Version:** a translation of the Bible from one explanation to another for a better understanding of the word of God.

**W-Wisdom:** the ability to judge correctly and follow the best course of action based on knowledge and understanding.

**X-Xersex:** the Greek name of Ahasuerus the King mention in the book of Esther known as Xerxes the Great. He was the King of Persia from 486-465BC.

**Y-Yahweh:** Yahweh, Elohim, names of God

**Z-Zeal:** Eager, having desire and enthusiasm.

Annie M. Burton

## **Children are Gifts from God**

Report these things to adults if you find yourself in any of these situations. You may also report to your teacher or counselor, parent, police, or any other authority figure.
Abuse: Verbal, mental, sexual, bullying

Kidnapping: any attempt of a person to take you away.

Car Jacking

Thoughts of Suicide

Domestic Violence

Thoughts of running away

Sex Trafficking

Teen Pregnancy

Thoughts of harming yourself

If you are in danger, yell, scream, call for help. Do not hesitate to tell anyone you see. Run. Your life is precious. God is the giver of life. You are very precious and powerful. You can put a stop to anything that's trying to happen to, you Be positive. Don't be a casualty. God loves you and your family and friends love you too. Do not smoke, do drugs, or drink alcohol. Resist sexual advances, resist peer pressure.

## **My Friend, CeCe**

I have met many people in my life, but non like my friend CeCe. We became friends right away. After graduating from nursing school, I began working at the hospital in my hometown. I had worked in several areas before transferring to that department. This is where I met my friend. I began orientation right away. I met the others, and we developed a good working relationship. We all were full time employees with two weeks paid vacation and sick days.

I noticed CeCe was taking more vacation days than anyone else. I asked her how she did it. She wouldn't tell me, so I stopped asking. Every two to three months my friend would go on vacation. This went on for a long time.

CeCe became ill and was admitted to the hospital for a long time. Once she finally got better and was released, she started going to church. She gave her life to the Lord. She like to give gifts to everyone. She was so special. She became ill again and was diagnosed with cancer. She was unable to return to work this time. We talked a lot while she was going through her illness. She was confessing the wrongs she had done.

She began telling me a lot about her life. She began talking about those vacations she used to take. They were not vacations at all. She was working in abortion clinics in different cities and states making a lot of money aborting babies. CeCe thought about the decisions she had made. She would schedule flights and get her plane tickets ahead of time. As time went by her condition worsened. She was miserable.

She said she could hear babies crying all of the time. Also, she could see babies faces everywhere. She could see faces in the clock, in the mirrors, in the hallway, the corner and even in flowerpots. She said she could not get any rest from seeing the babies. Different people would visit her home to take care of her.

Sometimes the decisions we make have consequence that affect our lives forever. I am praying that the law is changed, and Roe v. Wade will be overturned and stop the shedding of innocent blood. This is one of the seven things that God hates.

The blood of aborted babies cries out to God. I'm praying that Roe vs Wade be overturned and the shedding of innocent blood stops. When we make a decision, we want to make the correct one. If we don't there are consequences. People can suffer from consequences be careful about the decisions you make. They can affect you, your family, your life, and the people around you.

## **Courage and Social Justice**

In August of nineteen sixty-three I moved from Coahoma County Rural to Clarksdale my hometown. I had been a sharecropper on a farm. That year I decided to do better. I didn't finish harvesting the crop. I laid it by and left the farm.

I found employment at an Italian restaurant and began working the night shift. The work was not hard at all. I was a kitchen helper. I made salads, washed dishes, and cleaned up the place. At that time minimum wage had not been established or put in place. Even so it was work and I had some income. At first, I lived with my aunt, my mother's sister until things got better.

One day I went to the courthouse to register to vote. They told me I could not register until I paid a poll tax for three years. I needed to save my receipts for proof. The tax was three dollars per year.

Three years past and I went back to the courthouse to register to vote and brought my receipts. They gave me a test and put me in a vault so I couldn't copy and cheat. I failed the test the first time. They told me to try again. Every time a person attempted to register to vote their name would be posted in the local newspaper. Everyone who read the news would know about you. After a while I tried again and passed the test. My name went into the paper again.

My boss read my name in the paper and talked to me about it. There was a nationwide movement to get people registered so they could vote. The president at the time was John Kennedy. He was working on the Civil Rights Act. There were other presidents before him who tried to get it passed but couldn't. President Kennedy met his untimely death in Dallas, Texas in November 1963 by assassination. Mr. Johnson who was the vice president was sworn in as president. So, in 1964 the Civil Rights Act was passed into law by President Lyndon Johnson.

There was a movement all over. The Freedom Riders and different groups helped set up local people to march in the streets. Dr. M. L. King said no violence. In 1964 there was a march in my hometown, and I was employed at the Royal Funeral System. My boss's wife called and said, "Get ready and go join the march." I asked her who was going to run the funeral home. She said she would be there. When she came, I left to go join the march.

So, they had been marching for two days and I came in on the third day. Things were not so good the first two days. The police were there with their German shepherd dogs and Billy clubs. The firemen were there with their water hose. I drove my car to find where they were marching. I had a '54 Plymouth blue on blue. I found a park and told the marchers I came to join in. I don't remember what my sign said, but it had a slogan on it. One slogan was "Don't buy gas where you can't use the restroom."

It took courage to join the march not knowing if I

would be arrested or able to return home. When I left work. My family did not know I was there. The third day the march was quiet and peaceful. The police were not there with the dogs. The firemen were gone with their water hoses. We marched on the downtown streets singing the old Negro Spirituals on First Street, Second, Third, Front, court, Issaquena, and some side streets. After the march was over, I returned to work.

The Civil Rights Act was not only for African Americans, but for everyone who was discriminated against. The Italians could not have membership into the country clubs. This means they could not play tennis, swim, play golf, or have recreational activities. The African Americans could not have membership either. Everywhere was segregated. Two bathrooms, one white the other colored. We could not eat in restaurants. We could buy the food, but we had to take it outside. The doctor office had two waiting rooms. The water fountains were labeled for white or colored. Even the hospitals separated the races.

After the Civil Rights Act was passed the minimum wage began at $1.60 per hour. Things were getting better because people were making a little more money. Although fifty-seven years has passed since then, there is still much more to be done. We live in the best country in the world. That's why people from other countries want to come here to live and make a better life for themselves. We have a democracy for all people. We will overcome.

Annie M. Burton

# **Resurrection Day Song**

Play by Annie M. Burton

**Props needed:**

A Crown

A Red Broken Heart

30 Pieces of Silver

5 Halos

5 Angels

Drumbeats

**Female Roles**
Mary
Mary Magdalene
Salome
5-Angels

**Male Roles**
Jesus
Moses
Elijah
Peter
Andrew
James
John
Thomas
Matthew
Bartholomew
Simon
James
Phillip
Thaddaeus
Judas

## Zebedee

*The drummer begins beating the drums-*

Jesus was born in due time to save the world from sin. Born by the Holy Spirit, and He's coming back again.

Jesus had twelve disciples, but Judas sold him out for thirty pieces of silver. He didn't know what it was all about.

Sing Chorus-                                              Yea Sing
He arose

Jesus gave his life on Calvary out on that hill. He gave his life between two thieves, so we don't have to be lost.

When the earthquake had shaken the Temple, veil was torn in two. Where were all the disciples? I want to know where were you?

Sing Chorus-                                              Yea Sing
He arose

Peter, James, and John they were the favorite ones. Jesus took them to mount Transfiguration. They met Moses and Elijah on top of that mountain. There was a tabernacle and God met them too.

Sing Chorus-                                              Yea Sing
He arose

Thomas had a doubting spirit. He did not believe unless

he sees the nail prints in his hands. He was not at the scene.

Andrew, Matthew, James, and Simon too. Phillip, Bartholomew, and Thaddeus where were you?

-Sing Chorus-                                                    Yea Sing

Mary the mother of Jesus had a broken heart, to see her son die on that cross, it tore her heart apart.

Mary the mother of Jesus, she was standing at the tomb. His body was buried for three days. He arose as he said.

It was early one morning about the break of day and angel came from heaven and rolled the stone away.

-Sing Chorus-

He arose

He arose

He arose from the dead.

He arose

He arose

He arose from the dead.

He arose

He arose

He arose from the dead

And the Lord will take his children home.

What about the other Mary? Mary Magdalene, she was at the scene. Jesus cast seven devils out of Mary, and she never ever was the same.

*More drumbeats-*

> Yea sing

Sons of Thunder...

Sons of thunder..

What are you going to do with the sons of thunder?

I want to know where were you?

Zebedee, Salome

What are you going to do with the sons of thunder?

I want to know where were you?

Sons of thunder...

Sons of thunder...

Zebedee and Salome

Asking special seats in heaven that's not prepared for you.

He arose

He arose

He arose from the dead.

He arose

He arose

He arose from the dead.

He arose

He arose

He arose from the dead

And the Lord will take his children home.

Annie M. Burton

## **About the Author**

I am a living witness that you do not have to live I poverty. I was a sharecropper on a farm. That is the way it was at that time. I lived in a farmhouse on a plantation owner's farm. The owner did not charge rent or utilities. Beginning in January of each year I would get twenty-five or thirty dollars a month until August. I chop the cotton, keep the field free from weeds and grass. So many acres were assigned to me. Sharecropping was a form of slavery.

August is the month when the crop matures, and the cotton bowls began to grow. After the bowls mature you pick the cotton with your hands and it's weighed and at the end of harvest season. It goes to the gin then the compress. At the end of harvest the plantation owner gets one half and I got the other. All of the expenses came out of my half. Sometimes I would get the value of three to five bales of cotton valued from one hundred-sixty-five to one hundred-eighty-five dollars each. It all depends on how many bales of cotton your crop produced.

So, in August 1963 I laid my crop by. That means I released it back to the landowner after keeping the grass and weeds cut until harvest. You could do that. I left the farm, and moved to my hometown in Clarksdale, MS. I found employment at an Italian restaurant and began working the night shift. I went from sharecropper to the Italian restaurant, private home, delicatessen shop, nursing assistant.

I became licensed and bonded as an insurance agent for Security Life Insurance Company, to the royal Funeral System as secretary. Next, I applied to go to nursing school and was accepted in 1970. I graduated in 1971. After graduation I was employed at the local hospital until I retired in 1998. After living in Clarksdale for forty years I relocated to Horn Lake, Mississippi. I became a member of Christ Agape C.O.G.I.C. Pastored by Elder Albert Pass, Superintendent, and Evangelist. Under his leadership I enrolled into MAAI the Missionary Academy at the Headquarters Jurisdiction in 2005. I graduated two years of studying at the academy and the Mason Bible College under the tutelage of Dr. Peggy Harris and others. My church was under this Jurisdiction. Superintendent Dickerson L. S. Wells. Our Bishop was J. O. Patterson Jr. and He pastored Pentecostal Temple.

I have been an Evangelist Missionary since 2007. I'm a prayer warrior and intercessor. I am saved sanctified and filled with the Holy Ghost and soul winner for the

Kingdom of God.

I am currently a member of the Body of Christ. My church home is The St. James Temple Church of God in Christ Pastored by the Honorable Elder Willie George Bays Jr. with Lady Faith Bays at his side.

I give God the credit for my life. In everything to God Be the Glory for the things he has done.

I recommend this book to be used in churches as educational tools to educate children and others in and outside of the Body of Christ.

# Intervention Crisis Hotline Numbers

In case of any emergency dial 911

**Aids 24hr Hotline**
1-800-342-2437 Spanish 1-800-344-7432

**American Cancer Society**
1-800-227-2345

**Alcohol Tobacco Firearm**
1-800-283-4867

**Child Abuse Hotline**
1-800-25-ABUSE

**Child Find Investigation Location and Runaway**
1-800-426-5678

**Child Help USA Hotline**
1-800-422-4453

**Drug and Alcohol Info. National Clearing House**
1-800-662-4357

**Compulsive Gambling National Council**
1-800-522-4700

**Poison Control Hotline**
1-800-222-1222

**STD Hotline**
1-800-227-8922

**Sexual Assault Hotline**
1-800-656-4673

**National Suicide Lifeline**
1-800-784-2433

**Drug Overdose Hotline**
1-877-651-1690

**Center for Disease Control and Prevention**
1-404-778-2700

**Adoption Hotline 24hr**
1-601-960-8649 or 1-800-982-7395

**COVID19 Hotline**
1-866-211-5320

**Diabetes Hotline**
1-800-229-2559

**Domestic Violence Hotline 24 hrs.**
1-800-799-7233

## Contact Information

Annie Burton
2005 Center St
Clarksdale, MS 38614

sisterburton1@gmail.com

662-392-2869

662-985-8452

Available at all online retailers

Barnes and Noble
Amazon
Walmart
Books-a-Million
And more

Annie M. Burton